At

THE

LEPIDOPTERIST'S

HOUSE

Also by Chelsea Woodard

Vellum
Solitary Bee

At the Lepidopterist's House

Chelsea Woodard

Winner of the 2022 Michael Waters Poetry Prize

Published by the University of Southern Indiana
Evansville, Indiana

ISBN: 978-1-930508-55-2   First Edition

Printed in the USA

Library of Congress Control Number: 2023943220

This publication is made possible by the support of the Indiana Arts Commission, the National Endowment for the Arts, the University of Southern Indiana College of Liberal Arts, the USI English Department, the USI Foundation, and the USI Society for Arts & Humanities.

Southern Indiana Review Press
Orr Center #2009
University of Southern Indiana
8600 University Boulevard
Evansville, Indiana 47712

sir.press@usi.edu
usi.edu/sir
Ron Mitchell, Rosalie Moffett & Marcus Wicker, eds.

Cover image: Chelsea Woodard; *Bliss Lane House*
Cover design: Sheana Pickard
Layout: Macy Broshears & Zach Weigand

CONTENTS

I. Collectors

II. Mementos

III. Ephemera

IV. Anomalies

V. Resting Places

In later years, I rediscovered the same precise and silent beauty at the radiant bottom of a microscope's magic shaft. In the glass of the slide, meant for projection, a landscape was reduced, and this fired one's fancy; under the microscope, an insect's organ was magnified for cool study. There is, it would seem, in the dimensional scale of the world a kind of delicate meeting place between imagination and knowledge, a point, arrived at by diminishing large things and enlarging small ones, that is intrinsically artistic.

–Vladimir Nabokov, *Speak, Memory*

When I walked out the door, I knew everything I left in that house I'd be leaving for good. Most of it was easy to leave. But my medicine box, the one his dad had made for me, my fan, my gourd, my cedar bag, my shawl—these I'll have to learn to leave over time.

–Tommy Orange, *There There*

−I−
Collectors

Articulator

From skeletons awash in brackish shoals
and old bones, coated with slime, afloat
in shallows, you're tasked to visualize
a form: sperm or North Atlantic right,
their flukes months gone, their teeth
and baleen clinging now to scattered
shards of jaw, the jigsaw puzzle you'll assemble
piece by piece and hang in stale museum air.
In slow waves they will swim again,
a dorsal fin sticking straight up, a skull
dreaming of water and still dripping oil—
once harvested by seamen sick for home,
the hollows spermaceti-stained, a rill
spilling like tears. Certain assemblies
will take years, and when you've strung them
from the vaulted gallery, each vertebra
aloft, properly linked at last, you hope
you've raised some remnant of the past—
each segment in its place, a voice holding
the true expression of its shape.

Portrait of the Collector as a Young Man

I can scarcely manage to scribble a tolerable English letter. I know that I am not a scholar, but meantime I am aware that no man living knows better than I do the habits of our birds.
        –John James Audubon

When I came to the woods, I knew the ferns
were full of longing. Far from the bells
and white-fenced greens of towns, I have learned
the pardon of mosses, taking up spent shells

that glitter on the shade-dark earth like gold
fillings. Weightless as a carcass
free of flesh, my pack holds
spare instruments: a compass

and charcoal sticks, oil pigments, brushes.
My gun is a light, cold metal rasping
in its leather sleeve. Parting bulrushes
encircling a pond, I gasp

as a bittern lifts, ruffles the surface and squawks
toward the tree line. The bones
of a loon aren't hollow; no body that walks
can know what it is to skim alone

the tops of hemlocks, to see the sun rise
from a nest of dry branches afloat
in a pine. I wake to the eaglets' cries,
study my sketches, letters I wrote

home to Lucy. What brought me to this place
was not their plumage, alizarin
and ochre, nor a man's arrogant race
against where time will drive him—

no. It was the patterns of their flight—
great swooping arcs, marvelous shapes that glide
and shrink to black. The canvas's white
expanse is where their glory hides.

And so I've reimagined all the birds
as silent, stationary things
that cannot render viewers wordless
at the rustle of their wings.

Female Collector

Story hoarder, keeper of notes folded
in Latin class, stubs of dulled drawing pencils,
bits of wool sheared from the neighbor's ewe
(dyed pink or glossy white, like pearls),
drawers full of music boxes, the petty feuds of girls
(detailed in journals: grade 2, grade 9), coins

unearthed from extinction: Swiss francs, lire.
An entire life is possible to fold
away. The adolescent faces of girls
you grew up with: round, blonde-framed, penciled
in a litany of proms and first dates, adorned with pearls
worn by mothers and grandmothers. This older you

savors the dusty film forcing a U-
turn back to that time abroad, Cyrillic alphabets and rubles
pocketed as proof you watched the Neva purl
against its banks, that you never once folded
your hand when it came to risk. The future pencils
in a calendar filled with the birthdays of girls

now in their thirties, swaddling baby girls
who stare from photographs, their wide eyes trying to figure you.
So many dried tubes of paint, so many saved pencils—
graphite and charcoal, white. They are precious as coins.
Here is a cigar box of shells; here is a flag folded
by somebody. Three separate sets of heirloom pearls.

The needles your mother used to teach you *purl
one*—all those uneven stitches a girl
has to learn. Bright colored paper folded
into origami cranes; the names of those you
once loved creased, faded by time, marked
by post stamp, scribbled in archival pencil.

The vision locks on a self-portrait drawn in pencil,
your own eyes bodiless, black-centered pearls
that swim up through the dark like Krugerrands
sunk in a shipwreck. This is the record of a girl's
lost treasure, long stowed and loaded onto U-
Hauls, settled in closets, shelved and refolded

every time she's had to fold. Now the rain is pounding
luminous pearls on the glass; now another you
smudges the pencil features of the girl.

Jacob Grimm

Like children's fingers, branches grow thick
        and close, interlocked—
        here, in the heart
of the wood, where the mosses
        have crept over bones,
cloaking their slow decomposing
        with green. The moss gives a soft light

when the moon is gone. Numberless months
        I have hushed
        with my ear to the hole-
mouth of an oak, sifting darkness
        for sound. Some old stories curl
beneath last autumn's leaves, pickled
        by dank earth—their dry roof

rustling now from the clumsy breath
        of my feet. The world
        is a mouth waiting to murmur
its name. My brother and I are but vagrants
        who tramp through this dim hibernaculum—
half-starving for small crumbs, the timbre
        of moonbeams.

Herding Dog

Sheep pose a problem
of order. They bob

over a rock
when she blocks

their route to the fence
where they'd cluster, tensed

for the next pass.
The world is blurred grass,

the stink of mud
and dung, hooves thudding.

Hers is the rapture
of work that's entrenched

in long shoulders,
gazes that hold

the rabble still.
Her body is will

spilling right
to the edge. No biting,

no audible sound,
she sweeps around

the pen to head
off a yearling. She dreads

the days at home,
bronze eyes combing

the yard for straggler
geese, the flags

of half-dried towels
ruffling the deck prowled

hourly for squirrels.
Her paws quiver

when she dreams—
another gleaming

field, another
ripple of

taut muscle twitching,
the handler's switch

brushing a flank,
low springy banks

of clover. She walks
through mosquitos flocking,

ears pricked
at beetles ticking

after dark.
Her face is starker

in the night,
its floating whiteness

like a ghost
watching the house.

Emily Dickinson's Herbarium

Wide-lobed threes of trillium leaves taped
and labeled, trifoliate veins, wrinkles dried
and finite as her penciled marks beneath.
My hands are attuned to the weight of pages pressed
long on such fragile anatomies—pistils of lilies,
cowslip petals, delphinium halos and bright spikes
of iris, ovaries and ovules tenderly picked,
patterned and splayed. I know the body

of desire could fill a book and still spill
out. It isn't a question of will, or killing
for pleasure, for beauty that's flattened and lasts past
the end of one season, where we've lived in bloom
and hate to leave. Late February casts
its defeatist light—I quit this reliquary now, this room.

Metal Detectorist

Most days, I go out to the fields
before the sun comes up. It is half-light.
It is the time when phoebes puff
up on their nests, when the night

hasn't yet left its dreamers. Tall grasses
curve under the dew when I climb
the steep hill by Smith's lane where I found
my first relic. There was a time

when Mollie woke early, went hunting
along with me, when our children were young
and the morning seemed ready to spill
over the soft bedclothes they'd flung

off and wake them. My father uncovered
a hoard at eighteen, right there in Hemming's
pasture. His stories were ingot-filled,
brimming with bullion and neck rings,

the intricate smith work of Vikings. I hear
his voice in the knolls as I lower
my seeker—Time mowing the sun
with his scythe; I imagine I tower

above buried conquerors' plunder
as I put on my head phones and clutch
tightly my pinpointer. My father
tutored me to listen for the *touch*

of God, the ping that signaled treasure.
I found a rivet once, a silver hilt
inscribed with crosses—the mud-rimmed
wreckage of a world somebody built.

The Hagiographer's Reply

My skin is pale from summers spent
hunched in the dimming must

of special collections, donning cotton gloves
as I handle the pages. My days are solitary,

and almost no one understands the call
to what I do. Sometimes, I catch my neck bent

at odd angles, as if I've been riddled
with arrows, Sebastian-like, or hacked

with a knife—Cecilia's botched
beheading, Edmund's head rolled in the soft paws

of wolves—and I immediately straighten
at my work. Why harp on death?

Before they found the way, their lives
were commonplace—cloth dyers

for parents, or noblemen; women never wanting
to marry. I picture Kevin alone

between the lakes, in his chamber of stone,
Bega adrift on her turf raft—both resigning

themselves to the elements. Some of their bodies
stay intact; most visited by eager masses

of the faithful. But if I only wear their memories
as pendant charms, remember them

as they are now—granite and bone, patrons
of gravediggers or young girls—I've only made

another reliquary: commercial, incidental.
Here, in the cool dust of the library, their voices

summon from the old tongues: *clipian, vocatio*—
and as the daylight wanes, I listen, write

the living record of their names.

At the Lepidopterist's House

47 Bolshaya Morskaya Street, St. Petersburg

Their colors only fly by day. I always found
them trembling on leaves as chrysalids, flitting
from phlox to foxglove with new wings, soundless
in the thrum of early summer. I was sitting

on a bench on Nevsky Prospect once, waiting
for life to get exciting, when a monarch
broke the dullness of an iron gate
and tore the afternoon apart. One art

is like another. I wrote my sentences to show
slow phosphorescent motes and caught
my net on beauty. There's always more to know
about the world, the whirring light. Obsession taught

me patience, made me attentive to the shape
of thoraxes and microscopic veins, the bending
arc of stems. The killing jar is never where it ends.
Inside the glass, the vanished landscape

magnifies—its iridescent shades preserved in scales
that seldom fade in banishment or shame.
My ephemera are pinned, hanging from every wall,
though nothing ever stays the same.

The house front goes; the once opulent rooms
brim with the ravenous gaze of travelers,
and I myself am just a traveler whose vision zooms
in on the tiny fibers of my coat. Stitches unravel.

I once remembered all their names: skippers and coppers,
sulphurs and swallowtails. Their metamorphosis beguiles
me, and while I know the past will never stop her
badgering, I'll rest awhile inside their glorious disguise.

– II –
Mementos

In Memory of Pet Birds, Pandemic

Were the cages just barred windows
our family hung next to the kitchen windows
we all looked out of, safe in our little rooms
of glass and feathers? We shared the air
but they slept or ate or whistled suspended
from a tinkling hook in a hemlock beam, traveled
on gusts of trapped air from one sill
to another, drifting on wafts of steam
from the stove or the hot puffs of our breath.

Were the windows means for torture or
curiosity—cardinals and finches filched
of full song, settled in textureless branches, lifting
to clouded skies and cold winds raking
the undecided maples? The world is walled
with glass—a many-windowed room
we scour for smudges of dander, cracks,
cool drafts and leaves' thin shadows shifting
like the memory of wings across our faces.

Black and White Portrait

To a classmate on her 34th birthday

In the photograph, you're looking through
the balcony railings at St. Mark's.
We must have been crouching; you must have been watching
the Venetian crowds, large patches
of blue amid the clouds. The contrast is stark:
your profile set against shadow-hued
pillars; your blonde hair shows as white;
your sun-washed face and eyes lighter

than stone—colorless marble. Last year
I learned that you had died. I found
this relic from our term abroad—
bleeding sunlight, impossibly bright.
Somewhere behind the square a gondolier
is steering underneath the arcs
of bridges, soundless as he glides
between the shafts of dark and light.

Freeze Line

The angling settlement has been shut up
        for months, and all this time we've shuffled

timidly on shifting ice, watching
        the sky, the porch thermometer, missing

the dry wood creak of dory oars, the sun.
        Anxious for spring, we saw the thawing balsams

as a sign we had come through, wintered this last,
        cold-growing sorrow. Today we coast out

to the mouth of the river, past the eagle's nest
        and pools broken by deadheads, where the silt sets

rust-like on the banks and the lake rests, washes
        over algae-slick rocks. I watch

the wheel rasp under your palms, knowing you watch
        for rocks, shallow spots, the darker patches

showing wind—warnings that have been passed
        down over a lifetime. Fly rods catch dust

on the camp rafters. Soon, fishermen
        will come back to these waters; fathers will show

their sons to tie flies, to cast toward the drowned
        line of trunks, where branches stop, where ice swells

the banks and the cold writes its name on the land.

Painting I

9.11.01

Transcribe: to write across

The print is Japanese. I copy it—
transcribe, my teacher says; I'm striving to match
the washed-out colors of the ink, the luster
of the woman's hair. The easels lean
in a large circle, each of us facing out,
sharing our backs, eyes locking on the woodblock
figures that we try to catch
at bathing, staring vacantly in mirrors.
This is the way it starts: the windows watch
us while we squint and dab; fluorescent lights
flicker above our heads, abuzz like summer, like the end
of songs. Somewhere the static stops.
The radio announcer's voice washes
the likenesses like cadmium
that bleeds into the cool, watery hues we tried
so earnestly to render; they slip like breath
under our brushes poised to draw
those distant shapes that have already been imagined—
speckles of demons, or of birds,
tiny and black, scribbling in ash across a paper sky.

Christmas Pageant

We stashed the click-on candles
underneath the green felt stage
of the sanctuary, and held our breath

until the soloist had hushed the pews
packed with the faithful or nostalgic
children and grown-up children, home

this weekend for the spectacle, the snow.
All eyes locked on the empty cradle,
on the stairway door where this year's Mary,

eighteen and blushing, would appear
on my ex-Catholic father's arm.
Twelve winters in a row, he grew

the beard my mother hated, dressed
in Joseph's desert robes and wore
his solemn countenance across

the stage floor as he told jokes
to make each nervous Mary laugh.
I watched just one year from the dais,

at last the right age to be angel, to glory
in the long white robes that danced
what we'd only rehearsed in perfect silence.

We were not believers, Jews on my mother's side,
my image of the baby still the plastic doll
I'd long ago snuck up to see. Now, mostly,

I go to be among the audience, the family
and friends that I no longer know.
The choreography's the same, the choir's voices

I remember sharp as the frost
crusting the sills, the sudden updraft
from the heating grate snagging my breath,

                                 making the fake lights flicker.

Nostalgia

At seven, the sadness was grave, like a dove
      in spring half-dark wringing
the light from it. I had known little
      of grief—having been allowed
muggy stretches of aimlessness, love,
      the slow buzzing passage of stings
from sharp grasses and bees—the grim rattle
      held off by a riot of wildflowers

drowning its song. It began as an art
      for remembering: larch needles
and doll clothes, a wing from a moth—a pattern
      unbreakable now, held still in the mouths
of propped windows. Curtains part.
      In the road, a girl pedals
home, and the low metal creak of the lantern
      is blooming I can't get out.

Ruminant

Cud-chewer, ambition-lacking ambler
through spring pastures, mud stuck
to your udders and split hooves—
your body's always as it was. What does
it mean to have the grass as grass
again, the hay as mushy hay, the strands
of cellulose your yellow tile teeth
chomp on? I understand too well
the urge to spit back up, to taste
the bitter tang of bile in the throat,
sour coating the tongue—imagine grinding
out the chaff of sorrow, the indigestible
grit of so many frustrations. I'd be content
to dawdle, sway-backed, with my nose
close to the backside of my brother,
knees grazing eroded stone and new clover.
Content with the horns, eyes set wide
to the sides of the head to gaze out over
perennial dangers, horizons of marsh.

Fjord

For Marie

The day was bitter and gray, though it was late
summer when we boarded the tourist boat
in matching sweaters we had just bought at the market
and thin windbreakers, because we hadn't thought
to pack anything warmer. The sea pleated
in gusts that whipped past iPhones zoomed in on the stark
Nordic houses—clean crimson and white—dotting
dark patches of spruces, narrow fields at the edge

of the inlet. You were newly pregnant—only three
weeks—and your body so slender I wondered where
there was room, hoped for you, that this time it would stick.
We asked another passenger to take our picture
against deck railings, the backdrop of thick trees
where the water was blue and inscrutable, too deep to dredge.

Home Inspection

I had to hide our laundry when they came
to scuff their boots on the foundation, stick
a pocket knife into a beam to check
for rot, patrol the cellar for mold and comb

the crawl spaces. There wasn't any time
to get our things in order, so I shoved
the unread mail into the cupboards, shelved
stacks of books and tried my best to tame

the lawn that hasn't grown the way it should.
We cannot see the trusses anymore.
The sheetrock's in, and the gleaming maple floor's
already scratched. We didn't know the pale wood

molding would grow darker in the sun,
that we would only use the stove for one
short winter. The logs you split molder in cords
by the edge of the driveway. I have no words

anymore. Not for the man who calmly checks
off boxes. Not for the windows or the deck.
Not for the lilacs that return every June
to the little yard on which we've turned our backs.

−III−
Ephemera

Ice Out, Pandemic

The evening was awash in silver panes, drifting Pangea-like across the swelling
     water. Water surges from a spring in the clearing where I crouch with my
     5-gallon bottle

to carry home, where the morphing lake still harbors bald eagles and loons that
     float large at the edge of our beached dock. There have been moments of
     stillness before, when I felt beached

like winter-rocked driftwood or cracked hulls, ice-gnawed moorings and the
     frayed ends of bow lines, where I felt as I do now through storm
     windows of warped glass when winter is past but the cloistering

lingers. I finger ice shards washed up against shore rocks, take pictures of fog
     and the faraway outlines of loons fishing or calling as we would call to
     each other over the cold and shifting surface

of our world. Our bodies are ruled by these squalls, coming out of the south this
     morning, pushing the last sheets of ice into splinters. I pick out slivers
     of old conversations, our faces through screens of metal and memory

and wonder if the world I woke up to this morning—open water, whitecaps
     and wind, the far shore clear—is what I dreamt, or if this dream we
     shared has made the known world unrecognizable.

Tornado Warning

There were no hills to block
the tract of sky that stretched
flat, like an enormous plate, or the top
of the ocean, in every direction
as I drove on never-ending loops
that wound around city sprawls
of subdivisions, strip malls painting
each commuter town the same.
My first time in North Texas,
I had a rented car, the steering
unfamiliar as the feeling that I would fall
off of the edge of something,
be flicked or sucked up like a fly
from a curved surface of glass, from a floor.
I had to concentrate on the weight
of my fat and muscle, denim and leather
grounding me to the pleather seat,
to the pavement that sped under
tires somehow keeping the whole parcel
of us anchored to the overpass
tethered by steel to the earth
and immoveable though it trembled
and bobbed and I had to remember
about pressure and tonnage, those slivers
of physics that didn't make sense
in a place that could swallow large processions
of cars that looked bug-like in distances
bluer than ocean, though the ocean
was so far away, and the straightaways
faded brown by the sun that was
bigger here, too, always out, always glaring.
The first couple of weeks, I would dream
of roads narrowed through dynamite-
cleared notches and steep granite ledge,
of woods hugging closely to guard rails.
When the sirens ballooned

on my way back from Chaucer one evening,
the heat rose from the sidewalk in waves,
and through leaves usually heavy
with starlings, I saw the sky
had turned green, like the *Wizard of Oz*
or a frog pond, and I pulled out my phone
to hear my friend say they were touching
down near her in Dallas, *touching
down*, like a pogo stick or a witch's broom—
those nimble things that made me
long to fly back home—and I walked
quicker under the hanging, uncuttable air,
under the trees that were silent the way
they'd never been, and locked my door
against danger or nature and stared
out at the street as the greening world
darkened. I stayed in my apartment
for hours after the warning
had cleared, and though some columns
had grazed parts of the West End everybody
was fine. This place was a stranger to me.
This wind that plucked things
that were fixed and unrooted them.
I ran my hands over wanderers' poems
and found each line was a well-walked road,
ink mooring the letters to paper,
to the book and the cherry desk I'd dragged
with me to Boston and Baltimore
and now Denton, Texas, bumping over
long roads in hot U-Hauls on my uprooted way
to some rented, impermanent room.
I lived for two years in that town
and never felt that it sheltered me, somewhere
I loved for journeying, for pilgrims' tracks
and oaks swollen with raucous black birds,
for walking slowly in virescent air
that harbored funnel clouds and unformed
poems, whale-roads and westerlies,
forces that made me scared to disappear.

Monarch

She doesn't come here anymore. Wind
waits. New thistle pushes through wet fields
where, once, the milkweed's generous leaves
abounded. Belief abounded here once, too:
the butterfly carried the spirit of my grandmother
over our graduation chairs and bridal veils, slats
of a split-rail fence, so she could stay with us—
this was the story from my mother, passed flower
to flower until our waiting mouths were full.

Double Portrait: Migraine

I.

My mother lies in the upstairs bedroom,
a pillow shielding her eyes from the sunlight
that pours through south-facing windows.
For hours, sometimes days, she swims
in darkness, in the merciless throb
of her own blood vessels that can't
narrow down. There is no talking, no loud
noises; vomiting or trips to the emergency room
sometimes when the pain dilates itself
into everything. In the back of her car,
in a small yellow cooler, she keeps a shot
in case of a headache that can never be
just a headache. Hormones, they say, or chocolate,
or anything. A needle in the thigh on the side
of a dirt road. As a child, I could never
understand how a body could turn on itself,
make her lie corpse-straight and as still
as the winter pond. I never knew when she might rise,
Lazarus-like, stagger down the steep
stairs into morning, dust the sleep from her eyes.

II.

The winter is witchy and my left wrist
and fingers feel like they're falling

asleep, weak when I try to type emails
and weaker still when I try to write

poems. The next morning my left thigh
is numb, and I struggle to walk

up the street, to balance in a standing pose
I know like the small mole on my jawline, like the smell

of the thaw. Some mornings, I can't feel a part
of my cheek. There's something wrong

with my head, but it won't hurt the way
it's supposed to, the way I remember driving

at night at nineteen, a stoplight searing
into my eyeball. There's something wrong

with my heart, it turns out. Something
so soundless, so inconsequential, it's been missed

all my life—in the stethoscope's ear, in a hollow
that won't ever close. All along there was a slip,

an upward strain of blood that never carried
far enough to make me hear it. But in this chimerical year,

I clench my teeth through reflex tests, an MRI—
until a doctor holds the ultrasound against my chest, finding

the fetal flaw that never healed, that kept
its secret to itself all of this time until my body

begged for me to listen to the part
that had always been wrong, to my heart

        writing and rewriting its name.

Cabbage White

Upside down on mustard buds or blooms
of nasturtiums, its tongue extracts a bead of nectar.
From its wings: smudged-charcoal ears
and ink-splotch eyes, blank faces, the gentle whir
that it is spring, of blossom-dotted
hedges, the thicket where a hunter spies
between the gauzy spaces of his net.

Tower

In the Minchiate Tarot deck, this card depicts two naked figures fleeing a burning structure.

After an argument

Running through the granite doorway,
we never turned to see the great room
burning. Our feet had calluses of char; the air
held the smell of singed hair—
your green eyes lashless, your forearms bare.

But the hillsides were still brimming spring.
Our smoke-clogged bodies bled black riverbeds
of stones, smooth and cool in a bather's fingers.
The fire has left a ring
of ashes on the grass. Lately, I sing

to hear the heaviness of sound
falling, to watch its fullness swell
and drop like rain. Your anger is like rain
that gathers around
the parched flowers, and mine is the ground.

Great American Sea Eagle

Audubon painted and classified this bird; however, it was never seen or recorded by anyone else. It remains unclear as to whether it went extinct, or never existed at all.

    –Currier Museum of Art

Each slender barb is drawn with pen.
There is the illusion of weight,
a heavy breast, the slightest grin
as the bird stares down her gated
horizon—the paper's edge, the frame.
On the museum wall
her details are collected. Her name,
like all the other birds that call

from wetland backgrounds, cross-hatched limbs
of hemlock trees, declares
its immortality—a gauzy scrim
obscuring doubt. She bears
her mythic heft with grace.
Vanished is the hand
that sketched her feathers, traced
each umber vane—that trapped her in a land

of extinct vision, where a plaque
hints that she wasn't real.
But her talons are as black
as river stones, her keel
truer to life than the eager chests
of those leaning to get a closer look,
tentative fingers pressed,
as on the pages of a book,

against the layer of air above
the glass. It is what's past
that's haunting in the dove's
song, mourning the last
glimmers of light, that leads the eye
beyond the static pose
to where her stately body rose
in an imagined sky.

The Cardinal

In memory of Claudia Emerson

Today is cold and so bright
    I have to squint at the high drifts, the light

purple-tinged, nearly unbearable as I walk
    back to classes, seeing tree trunks chalked

with smudging, soft lines of fresh snow.
    This year is tired and old, and I know

time only as the step between dark and sleep,
    the stinging breath I hold through the quick sweep

of sun brushing my face. I look through the glass:
    bare bushes, the dull birds who pass

through the frame and are gone. This time
    is like each time before. Through the grime

and plow sludge, the powder sky, he appears
    on the branch: crimson, fluttering, clear.

My husband thinks I've imagined him, that no bird
    like this comes here—but I've heard

him sing through dim afternoons, know
    he flies mildly, lighting the winter, goes

                    where we can't follow.

Coyote

Slinking through the brush
in the dip between two pastures,

she pauses to stare where we walk,
past the lowered heads of Holsteins

grazing, then turns to the north.
I've never seen one before, her fur

reddish in twilight, the same warm tones
as the grass. Her body is slight, her ears

pricked like the pet that sleeps
next to us, tail tucked, gaze gold-flecked,

feral, pointing where her quick movements
will follow. Trotting slowly uphill,

crossing the road where hay bales
thin in the soft clanking of cow bells,

she dissolves from our view. I heard
coyotes howling in packs as a child,

my cheek pressed to the bedroom window.
Bodiless, roaming night forests like ghosts,

their emptiness seemed like a hole
in the dark, sharp in the cold

cast of the moon. But here, the sun
cuts yellow edges on the tufts of field

turned up by hooves, and the wild dog
reappears where pine branches and bog

come together. Closer to shadows
now, she is as real as the stranger you know

as your own: wary and eager, a thief in your home.

– IV –
Anomalies

Fertility Clinic, Pandemic

I go alone and wear a mask
through the sliding glass doors.
I'd never have allowed myself to ask
these questions, not in the time before

I feared the sliding doors
might close for good. A stranger draws my blood
and asks my date of birth, but not before
she takes my temperature. I once stood

closer to a stranger than was good for me. My blood
is drawn from vials to test for FSH and estrogen.
The temperature in the memory I stood
in was too cold. The names of women

stamp the little vials—each will be tested. When
will we allow ourselves to ask
why it's so cold in this room where women
go alone, wear masks.

Rampion

In his fear, the man agreed to everything.
  —Jacob and Wilhelm Grimm, "Rapunzel"

To long for something is an ache
lodged in the deepest part
of the belly, an emptiness that feeds
on its own hollow—flattened and clenched—
like the inside of a tightened fist. It was
in this way that I pined for a child,
with this pang, this hunger.

So, when our little window opened
to the purple flowers below
the neighbor's wall, their spindly petals bled
into my dreams. I didn't care
about the cost: the letting down
of hair, lithe bodies falling
through the summer air.
I only knew the roots
had taken hold somewhere, and no tower
was too high, no threshold
dangerous enough to stop
my indehiscent want from blooming through.

Sita

For fourteen years, it was the forest
that I held, gathered around my shoulders
like a cloak, a blanket of bleached needles
that I walked on, barefoot, every day
we couldn't leave. No spell was forcing
us to stay, but when a father asks, his favorite son
obeys, and so we waited in the shade
of sandalwood and banyan, and I kept
count of everything: tubers and nuts we ate,
my monthly blood, the moon—my fingers
tightening on my mala. The myths don't talk
about the fire ants or the lice—snakeskins'
slow hissing through the underbrush. They like to say
that I was loyal, plot my path among soft
ferns and fragrant grasses, but the truth
is that I might have stayed in that wood,
with the leaf cover so thick no demon
jealousy could grow. I might have hidden
from the fate that had me only end two ways:
bound to my lord or burned. I could have fled
the story that depended on my rescue
to survive, as if I'd never seen the fire
brimming through the trees, the distant
shapes of islands looming. I hold
my parched throat open—tall water rising over ash.

Hypatia

Searching the constellations for a sign,
I walk the jetty in the June-damp air. The lecture hall waits;
the pressing hum of voices nearly stifles mine.

I look up always to the roof—ceiling or cirrus, star—my thoughts
are far off. Formulas are clouding up my head. The books
I've never read pulse in their shelves, and tiny dots

freckle the blue-black spaces of the sky.
Casting aside their distant god, I've picked fixtures
I can touch: the chart and astrolabe, the cry

of gulls swooping for fish, scales, planets that glitter, words.
Searching the constellations for a sign,
I miss what's written in the clouds, the falling shapes of birds.

Corvid

Grudge-keeper, harbinger
of the bad, black darter
in new grass, dull-billed and raucous
worrier, hoarse talker and tempter
of dogs and fed-up farmers,
keen swallower of rain-logged worms—
your caw nags at the edges
of sleep. You, who live a double life
and flock sometimes to one roost,
sometimes another—dark quill mark
at the margin—imperturbable
flapper that rasps like a cold frost,
like death. You are the restlessness
stored in my bones, a forecast
that claws from the half-murk of dreams,
reminder of blank spaces in leaves
and damp lichen; sly robber of low nests,
when I see you I see only bleak skies
and brown pastures, though the lawn is still teeming
with green, the clouds billowing summer.
Around the tucked wings of your brothers
shade gathers, and dry larches turn
murderous, soughing their prophecies.

Elijah and the Raven

The other stories are the same: cast into the uncertain chill
of the orphaned, the expelled, all God's abandoned
children are fed, not by their mothers or townsfolk, but from the bodies
of animals: those Roman brothers suckled by wolves, the Persian boy
born pale, saved by a monstrous mountain bird. In these myths,
what's most feared is made tame: the fanged she-wolf nuzzles; the raptor's
razor claws gentle, placing bits of flesh on the baby's tongue.

But for the grown man sent to the banks of the brook, ordered
to drink from its churnings, to whom the crow swooped
with scraps of bread, beef stolen from nearby farms—
the world was always plentiful: his place at the table set, the door
to the house held open. This was the way the thief had fed
him from its clever beak—so he would never know the damp
of a deserted nest, a bare-footed frost, the cold of folding-closed arms.

Portrait of the Artist as Failure

What / is man but his passion?
  —Robert Penn Warren, "Audubon: A Vision"

After A.E. Stallings

It started with an itch   to capture prettiness,
to set down and record   all that the sparkling world
forgot. There was a spot   at the edge of Stephansplatz

where vendors sold peaches.   My memory can't reach
that far—and the little hints   of yellow and alizarin,
while unconvincing, serve   as blazes of my fervent

pocketed desire.   At night, I dreamt of fire
along the Kärntner Strasse   somewhere I'd often pass
en route to other things.   In another age, kings

might have commissioned my work.   But now, in the settling dark
of the new century   Vienna's fine academy
wants none of it. I was   a boy who never blossomed

as he should. Mine was   a mind nevertheless resolved
to see its passions spring.   What happens when the thing
you love refuses you?   A painting gazes through

the scrim of time and asks   if beauty ever lasts,
if the miniature folds   in a woman's dress will hold
someone's attention, a stranger's   stare in some dim future,

in some other place—a wall   an attic corner. I'd give it all
to know that thrill again   proportion forming like a friend
on the blank paper's face.   There never was a race

to reach the vanishing point, the end.   A line should never bend
if the palace is to be   believed, if the standing body
really can hold weight.   To understand a shape

you have to set it in   motion; you have to squint
so that the colors blur   and all that lingers is the pure
expression of its heft, clean angles.   Inevitably, the vision tangles

focus in the real.   You must allow something to fall
into the dark it sprang from   even if it comes back wrong,
the landscape gone, the place   of all your dreams erased.

Exhibitionist

In the recurring dream
I had at thirteen, I'd return
to the shadowy time
when, caught in a stream
of gossiping teens learning
to steer clear of the limelight,
to incessantly point, *there*—
I looked down to discover
I'd worn a short skirt, and no underwear.
My body exposed, my modesty bare
to the cruel gazes of strangers,
shame pricked like the stare
of a crowd, an old lover—
the first bite of cold in October.

II.

At the end of a dead-end dirt road
where the trees widened to wet fields,
at the end of a long spring, in the garden
of childhood, we waded through weeds
and wet straw, past my mother's
tomato-staked rows, picking stalks
of asparagus. The feathery leaves
tickled our skin. We didn't know
any flaw in our nakedness then,
the power it yielded or gave up
to others. Through our toes,
the muddy earth squelched, the sun
warm and prickling our whiteness.

III.

The campus was empty and cold at the close
of Thanksgiving break, a lonely clock
tower tolling over the quad as I walked
back from the gym. I didn't encounter
a soul. Silent for once, the grackles
bunched close in the oaks, their bodies
obscured by thick leaves. The sky was the color
of old stone or dull metal, the brick
science building imposing. A loud thump, like a bird
flying hard into glass: he was framed
in the windowpane, naked, his fondling a blur
of pale skin when I started to run. It was as if I
was stunned from the crude fact of impact,
magnified in the range of a rifle scope—his,
the small, merciless eye at the other end of the lens.

Forest Bather

At first, the doctor told her she should stand
        under the canopy
for two hours, or as long as she could bear.
        It wasn't hard to flee

the overcrowded city, but the drone
        of cars followed her here,
and she could hardly block them out to listen
        to the pulsing fear

rising against her sternum. The forest floor
        was damp. She felt her pockets
for her office keys, her phone—purposefully left
        in her car—which was unlocked

at the pull-off. She watched an orange slug smearing
        itself across a log,
a red squirrel lifting its grip upwards.
        She'd left her yellow dog

at home, and so this solitude engulfed
        her like sublimated
fog from spring snows, like the evaporating dreams
        that were good, that she hated

to wake from. Oak saplings trembled when she brushed
        their branches. She had come
to be among things that couldn't speak,
        but the early morning thrummed

with chickadees and dried leaves, beetles and trillium.
        Over the years, she'd lost
her hold in the world, and she could hardly summon
        the memory of frost

sharp on her mother's garden, cool moonlight bleeding
        between birches. Breathing
was difficult sometimes. What was the silence
        pressing underneath?

Where were the words she needed to describe
        the robins' broken shells
and husks of garter snakes, the little spells
        when we escape our bodies?

Open Water Swimmer

For Craig

At first, your ankles tell you to get out,
he says, and on the dock, I understand
at once the natural tendency to flee
what is too raw, too deep. I dip my hand
into the lake: clear, cold as the sea.
Primitive, conserving, the body carries doubt
under its surface, in the nerves whose waves
roar in my fingers each time they thaw, revived

from freezing. Tireless, for weeks he swims
in salty coves, northernmost ponds, rivers
swollen in late spring, until the fat moves
just beneath the surface of his skin. Shivers
prickle my limbs that are still dry, still learning how to love
their reflex shudder when the distance brims.

In the Matter Of

In the matter of the plywood counters
that we ate our meals on for a year while we lived
in the unfinished house that we were building
for a year so many years and all those months
of rain on the high windows and new seeded grass
just coming in and slowly growing, bulldozed lilacs—
in the matter of the change of address in the town
we moved to just in time to leave, where I was born
and buried my father two Mays later in the matter
of the times we slept beside each other while the snow
fell heavy, deep outside the windows and our dog
snored, sprawled between us—in the matter of
the birthdays and the beard you grew, coffee
in bed, the matter of your father's last gasps
while we sat beside him in that room above the lake
and in the matter of your blond hair turning gray, your
green eyes darker in the matter of your body poised
mid-dive off of the dock into that stormy water
in the matter of your laugh, your crooked jaw, the matter
of the time our family watched us dancing by that lake
and in the matter of the ashes I will scatter there—
my father's, ours—the matter of the house
we couldn't save, unpainted cupboards—in the matter of the child
we didn't have, that little pit of sadness, in the matter
of our fathers and of roads we drove so often
in the matter of the eagles that would nest
above our first house in the matter of the favorite dog
we lay alongside while she took the needle in the matter
of the sun, bright on midwinter mornings in the matter
of the woodstove stoked so carefully the matter of
your heart and mine the matter of the distance
spread like last breaths in the matter of
a body that can't break itself the matter of what can never
be translated in the matter of the language lost
forever in the matter of the ice storm and black birches
just beyond the house the matter of the time spent

loving everything and not enough the matter of
two bodies slipping past each other in cold water
in the matter the boat floating across dark surfaces
the engine cut the matter of the stars, my father's voice
the matter of a constellation hard to make out in the matter
of the sky stretching its dome over the two of us
the matter of the water lapping scratched hulls
in the matter of the time it took us just to float here
in the matter of Orion and Andromeda the quiet night and loon song
in the matter of a voice too far to hear itself the matter of a voice
calling its afterlife the matter of the place we've drifted out into
the matter of this raft not mooring anywhere this water

– V –
Resting Places

Self-Portrait as Eris

I no longer comb my hair.
My tempers swirl in all directions.

Once meek, once carefully groomed
and caught in the gnarled grip

of manners, I have let fall
my girlish robes, holding

instead a small dagger, a chill
that sits at my hip, tethered

by air. I am the bitterness
rising like bile in the dry throats

of mourners, of spurned women
whose desire has grown tired,

whose loneliness whittles a hole
in the heart of the coveted apple.

I've rolled into the clearing, looking
golden and sweet. In the eye

of the sea-storm, at home, I will crouch,
wearing my old bones and sheltering nothing.

At Drumcliff

Co. Sligo, Ireland

The hazel wood was on the small map
from the tourist office, though I'd never thought
it was a singular place, rather some pause between the clap
of an August storm and a poet's mind knotted
with landscapes, songs. I came to find
whatever melody was left. Here, a small hill
rises from the town, the sycamores forming
a grove over the white and blackened headstones.

The summer morning is completely still.
My shadow's slight across this grave
I've come so far to stand above,
to take a long look, as from the pages
of a book I've kept for years to save
the worn inscription from a man I loved.

Wren's Nest

For Jill

The window of my sadness opened to a bird
boisterous and chirping from the back-porch lattice,
piling her cradle of twigs beneath the spread
of new leaves. It was spring, and the worst part
supposedly past, but the sunlight was scoring through spotless glass,
and there was no hanging roost where I could hide
under the shade of a roof, behind a screen
of geraniums. The flowers would slowly die.
Inside, I heard the hollow of my baby's cry
slice through the rooms. Sometimes I'd wanted to kill
the bird, uproot her brood that brought mildew and drought
to my plants, that, daily, squirming and pink, filled
my eyes with new blindness. Nature bred
pain. But then I saw, amid thin straw and birch down,
snippets of thread, where she had sewn
the cotton sacs of spider's eggs into the sticks;
by instinct, she had known the unseen
threat of mites, perils that lurked
within her chicks' own feathers, and so she wove
the greater danger underneath the fibers of her home—
holding that darkness close, keeping
her worry sharp against the things she loved.

At Cerveteri

Pulvis et umbra sumus.
    –Horace

In memory of Cynthia Bognolo

The mounds were grass-covered, rising from limestone
slabs, and we were camera and pen-clad, scouring
the streets of the dead. I'd never been to a necropolis,
though in your classroom we'd exhumed ghost echoes
of declensions, drowned hexameters, glimmers
Aeneas lost leaping from foreign sands,
our dog-eared grammar pages. This language never ages,
much like you—the tortoise shell clasping back silver hair, eyes sharp
above black dresses. But those interiors contained
stone beds, carved pillows, frescoes to usher love
into the rest that shimmers just beyond these earth-dimmed
corridors—some river of forgetfulness, some field
blooming with sound, Cerberus's wide mouths marking
the edge of dreams.

                I kept an envelope of photographs—
a relic long misplaced among the wreck
of twenty years—catching us sun-spotted, climbing
on the tombs, students and travelers, shadows
that dot our waking memory. *Fugit inreparabile*—a lesson
certain histories outlive even in burial, in myth.

Grave Ship

The Oseberg ship, thought to have been built around 820 A.D., was discovered in a Viking burial mound in 1903. Inside it, along with numerous artifacts, were the bodies of two women.

All of my underpinnings crumble.
Heaved into harsh Atlantic air,
I crave the dimness of my loam-hold,
no more heaving sides, the stillness
where no water is, no wind.

My prow has moldered; my masts
centuries lost inside a land
I'll never recognize—my planks
bereft of wetness, dry as the sand
on this pillagers' island.

They pry from me my mistresses'
prizes—beautifully carved, cleaved
from the same oak beams as I was.
We no longer belong
to these tidal pools; the undertow,

so often sculled away, harbinger
of tugging murk, of depths,
in this new age becomes us. The bight
waxes rich with the bleached bones
of my fleet-sisters—vessels deathless

even in rest—for there is no
harbor to anchor me
now that my shroud is shoveled out,
my ribbing removed
and my beached skeleton stoved in.

Buried under blue clay,
my hollow remembers
each doomed revenant of the sea,
every old body turning
to hull-shadow, filament, salt.

Sabbath

My father never calls it work
when he backs out the tractor
some damp April morning and motors
across the small road to the dairy farmer's
field. Two older cows dead in the night,
the herd waking, the large dome
of their bodies growing heavy, cold
in the first light, the ground
only recently thawed. They have an unspoken
arrangement. Out of some deep need
to help, some morbid concern
for the dead, the caretaking of burial
or of kind-hearted neighbors, my father, who perhaps loves
his tractor more than he loves
talking or gin and tonics, will never
say no, not to the friend whose hill
slowly erodes, to the widow who can no longer
mow her own pasture—not to the call
that comes early one Sunday
when the fog still hangs its chill
over the river, over the valley where
he digs the eight-foot hollows of their graves.

Krugerrands

For Betsy

Buried just behind the granite post
that marks the outline of my garden, the gold
grows colder. Its presence is my family's lore,
and like most myths, it seems fantastic, old;
some muggy August days it is a sore
that festers in the earth, or else it is a ghost
entombed below my heart—hepatic, dark.

All that the gate of love let in I've tried
to stone out—restoring toppled walls that littered
my pastures with feldspar and quartz—lost
fortunes. Blinded by bullion glitter,
we were naïve to what our secret cost,
and let the myrtle grow. Its rich leaves lied.
I can still see the heaving shovel's mark.

Book Mite

Little body in the pages
of a tome I've lugged around
with me for years—boxed up and banged
around in humid moving trucks, cast-off
in basements when there wasn't room
for the old volume that enclosed you,
fed you from its mildewed leaves. I took
my leave from you then, and took instead
a class in grad school where we learned
the names for *folios* and *quartos, recto, verso*—every
fold and fiber you've tucked the little sight
of you inside. I don't resent you,
friend—we are two travelers
hitched onto words in different typeface,
different blends of paper. We feed
on others' songs and on the rippled
texture of tear-moistened pages.
For now, you're hiding here, slipped
somewhere among my newly assembled
shelves. We have to take account
for ourselves. I'll find my way out later.

Apiary

Enclosed by thousands of eyes, my house
        emits a muffled buzz. The clapboards are painted

with faces of elves and saints, spindly trees
        in silhouette, foxes. No predator can threaten

here. Here, where the splintery walls purr
        woeful promises, where starlight filters

through cracks and bathes each waxy cell
        in a cold glow. I was born on a morning

in March when the bees pressed at the center
        of the hive to keep warm. It was still then.

Still as snow. But always I've felt a low drone
        at the heart, a small murmur that gathers

in summer and grows. I have flown
        down the keyhole. I have waded knee-deep

in the anther of roses, dark yellow, the color
        of every one of my filled, singular rooms.

Hedgehog

Dweller of edges
and of liminal lands,
estivator and eater
of mealworms, marker
of habitat trends
and imbalances,
protector of soft
underbellies, tunnel-
maker through rows
of immaculate bushes
near pastures and farms
you've pre-dated
by epochs with little need
to evolve—show me
the way one can stutter
and hiss at uncertainty,
ball up when a threat
becomes real, sleep
through unfavorable weather
with no food and no
light, just the specter
of pterodactyl wings
high above autumn-red
grasses and the sun's
deepening slouch
below the hills.

A Letter that Never Reached Montreux

I never visited your grave, though I've got my canceled ticket
from last August, a ferry chart, pictures of fields I imagined
brimming with Queen Anne's lace, the late knelling of crickets.

I don't know what it is to never go home, though, years ago, I looked
up at the arched ceilings your father owned, rows of glass
cases busy with specimens, once-treasured nets—I took

so many photos. I remember plummeting down
to the deep stations of the metro—gold carved columns and blue marble walls—
like buried treasure hoards or death chambers. In the little town

where I was born, my father rests under a white pine,
and he died like that, gazing up between evergreens
at a February sky. The winter is mine.

Summer never granted me the flight
I needed, though I watched herons, ravens and hawks,
butterflies whose names weigh down their lightness.

Those months, I found a kindness in the sun, a blessing
in its constancy. But in this season, it's the moon
that waxes, pearl-like, a naked woman dressed

in her own luminosity. I wore a pair
of wings last Halloween—lifting and black
at my back. I've seen your drawings and the air

sharpened by monarchs each September; I found
a luna moth sunning herself on hot pavement in the month
when my blood thrummed, when I never heard the roaring sound

of jet engines, the pop of my ears as we rose steeply
to elevations no live body could survive.
I want to tell you that I have loved deeply

in this world, that I have known the true weight of a heart
in a plummeting body, that I have learned how to scream
myself calm on the interstate, windows cracked, my throat finally starting

to open. I want to gift you that song, of dried grasses
windblown at roadsides, of lost flight patterns and homes
reconceived as this bright dream hurtles past us.

Acknowledgments

I am grateful to the editors of the following journals where these poems originally appeared, sometimes in earlier versions:

32 Poems: "Coyote," Herding Dog," & "At Cerveteri."

Asheville Poetry Review: "Wren's Nest" (Third Place, William Matthews Prize).

Blackbird: "At the Lepidopterist's House," "The Cardinal," & "Hypatia."

Birmingham Poetry Review: "Double-Portrait: Migraine."

Mezzo Cammin: "Portrait of the Collector as a Young Man," "Female Collector," "Tower," "Freeze Line," & "Nostalgia."

River Styx: "Articulator."

I am also grateful to Mikhail Iossel, who first introduced me to Nabokov's short stories as an undergraduate, and who afforded me the opportunity later on to travel to St. Petersburg and visit Nabokov's house and butterfly collection through a scholarship with his program, Summer Literary Seminars. I'm thankful to the Sewanee Writers' Conference and the support of a Walter E. Dakin Fellowship, which enabled me to begin some of these earlier poems, and to Pete Fairchild, for his generosity as a reader at that time. I'm grateful to many friends and colleagues for their input and support along the way, especially Tori Sharpe, Stephen Kampa, Courtney Sender, and Matt Miller; to Sheana Pickard for her beautiful cover design and lifelong sisterhood, and to Ron Mitchell for his care in editing this book. I have so much gratitude for my family, in all of its iterations, and for all of my teachers.

The Michael Waters Poetry Prize was established in 2013 to honor Michael's contributions to *Southern Indiana Review* and American arts and letters.

Previous MWPP Winners

2021—Bethany Schultz Hurst

2020—Erin Rodoni

2019—Julia Koets

2018—Chelsea Wagenaar

2017—Marty McConnell

2016—Ruth Awad

2015—Annie Kim

2014—Dennis Hinrichsen & Hannah Faith Notess

2013—Doug Ramspeck

Southern Indiana Review Press